Printed in the United States of America.

Published by D & B Press, a division of Doodle Books Publishing.

Author: Rachel Dunham
Editor: Deborah Kevin
Design: Rachel Dunham + Heather McNamara
Author Photography: Christa Meola, Jenny Moloney
Stock Photos: Stocksy.com

ISBN-10: 0-9909832-7-7
ISBN-13: 978-0-9909832-7-9

Library of Congress Control Number: 2017945634

Publisher's Cataloging-in-Publication Data is available.

Doodle Books Publishing
Barrington, RI 02806
www.DoodleBooksPublishing.com

www.YourBrandTherapy.com

this book belongs to

[RE] DISCOVER *yourself* [RE] DEFINE *your brand*

a series of *reflection exercises* to help you clarify your mission, who it's for, and how important *you are personally* to the success of this vision

JOURNAL

RACHEL DUNHAM

For my husband, Mike. Thank you for loving me even when I didn't love myself. Most people admire you for your profession – it certainly takes a special person to run into situations where everyone else is running out. But what I have found to be even more heroic is the confidence with which you've encouraged me to pursue my own happiness ... knowing the ripple effect that it will have on you, and our family. Your willingness to embrace uncertainty purely out of love for me is a testament to the person you are. Without you, I would not be me. For so much more than that, I love you. Deeply.

I'VE BEEN WHERE YOU ARE.

You're ready to embrace your growth. But that also means showing up — for better or worse — as the face of your business. And being your *true* self in front of the world.

BEING VULNERABLE ISN'T COMFORTABLE. BUT IT IS BEAUTIFUL.

Your clients crave that vulnerability. They want to know you've got their backs and can help them achieve stellar results. But they *really* want to know that you're human, too. Chances are, they have been questioning themselves as well. I encourage you to give them that vulnerability. Show them who you really are. *Be* your brand. Doing so will help you reach more of the people who need your brilliance – and have a greater impact on the world.

This journal is designed to guide you through a series of reflection exercises to help you clarify your mission, who it's for, and how important *you are personally* to the success of the vision.

There are a few givens in life and business. We don't have a ton of time here. There is so much beauty right now in this moment — in who you are at your core.

WHEN YOUR BRAND DOESN'T REFLECT AND EMBRACE YOU, YOU REALLY CAN'T FULFILL YOUR TRUE PURPOSE AND BE HAPPY.

I invite you to fully embrace who you are in the pages that follow. It is my hope that these reflection exercises help you finally feel comfortable and enough in your own beautiful skin.

Celebrating you and your brilliant vision,

Rachel

AT THE CORE OF
EVERY SERVICE-
BASED BUSINESS
IS **A PERSON.**

a beautiful, talented,
soulful person

As a spiritually connected entrepreneuer, it's likely that you started your business in an effort to better the lives of others, yourself, and your family. Many of us begin our entrepreneurial journey with a burning desire to help people, make a difference, and live a better life by doing what we love. All too often, as time passes, that deep passion to help, combined with the daily activities required for client fulfillment and growing a business, seem to slowly become the driving forces behind the business.

Particularly for solo-preneurs, running a business can feel lonely after a while. Sitting behind a computer begins to feel comfortable and safe; and before you know it, that clear driving passion you once had suddenly feels kind of muddy. What you *do* in your business has replaced why you do it and what you stand for. The service you offer is now driving your business, rather than your beautiful vision.

Naturally, with growth comes change. It's expected that your products and service offerings will need adjusting as your business grows. Price points will increase as you become more confident and offer higher levels of service to your clients. Your staffing needs will also adapt to your changing client base and business model. But, at the core of it all remains one constant. *You.* Beautiful, talented, caring, soulful, and perfectly imperfect you. Of course, with time you'll grow and evolve personally. But you are still you. And that is one of the key reasons why *you* are actually your company's greatest asset.

15

don't ask youself
what the
world needs;
ask youself
what makes
you come
alive
and then go and do that.
because what the
world needs
is people who have
come alive.

HOWARD THURMAN

DO YOU REMEMBER WHY YOU STARTED YOUR BUSINESS? WRITE ABOUT AND REFLECT ON THE REASONS WHY YOU DID.

WHAT WERE YOU YEARNING FOR? WHAT WAS APPEALING ABOUT OWNING YOUR OWN BUSINESS? WHAT WAS YOUR TOP GOAL FOR THE BUSINESS THAT FIRST YEAR (WHETHER FINANCIAL, EXPERIENTIAL, OR OTHERWISE).

18

19

DO YOU REMEMBER "WHO"
YOU WERE WHEN YOU FIRST
HAD THE IDEA TO START
YOUR BUSINESS? DO YOU
FEEL LIKE THE SAME PERSON
NOW?   .

NATURALLY WE ALL EVOLVE.
20 WE GROW. WE DREAM
BIGGER AS TIME PASSES.

HOW HAVE YOU GROWN AND
EVOLVED PERSONALLY FROM
WHEN YOU FIRST OPENED
YOUR BUSINESS? AND, HOW
HAS THAT GROWTH AND
EVOLUTION SHIFTED YOUR
BUSINESS DESIRES AND
DIRECTION?

21

though we travel the world over to find the

beautiful

we must carry it with us, or we find it not.

EMERSON

WHAT ARE SOME OF THE
QUALITIES THAT YOU LOVE
ABOUT YOURSELF?

WHAT MAKES YOU BEAUTIFUL?

reflections

27

note

SOMETIMES IDENTIFYING QUALITIES THAT WE LOVE
ABOUT OURSELF CAN BE CHALLENGING. THINK ABOUT
WHAT CHARACTER TRAITS AND QUALITIES OF OTHERS
YOU MOST ADMIRE. OFTEN THOSE QUALITIES WE ADORE
IN OTHERS ARE A REFLECTION OF WHAT WE LOVE ABOUT
OUR OWN BEAUTIFUL SELF.

YOU LIKELY STARTED YOUR
BUSINESS WITH A VISION.
WHAT WAS IT? RECALL AND
REFLECT ON THAT.

DO YOU REMEMBER YOUR
ORIGINAL ELEVATOR PITCH?
WERE YOU CONFIDENT
28 INTRODUCING YOURSELF
BACK THEN?

HOW DO YOU NOW
DESCRIBE YOUR SERVICES
TO NEW PROSPECTS OR
INTRODUCE YOURSELF AT
NETWORKING MEETINGS?

you have extraordinary treasures hidden within you. bringing forth those treasures takes work and faith and focus and courage and hours of devotion. we simply do not have time anymore to think so small.

ELIZABETH GILBERT

WE REFLECTED PREVIOUSLY
ON HOW YOU'VE PERSONALLY
EVOLVED SINCE STARTING
YOUR BUSINESS. NOW THINK
ABOUT HOW YOUR BUSINESS
VISION HAS EVOLVED SINCE
YOU FIRST LAUNCHED IT.

WHAT IS YOUR VISION NOW?

32

TAKE THE TIME TO GET
CLEAR AND WRITE IT OUT
HERE, EVEN IF YOU'VE
ALREADY DONE THIS BEFORE.
FOCUS ON THE BIGGER GOAL
YOU ASPIRE FOR. HOW CAN
YOUR BUSINESS HAVE AN
EVEN GREATER IMPACT?
AND, WHO DO YOU NEED
TO BE IN ORDER TO FULFILL
THIS DESIRE?

DREAM BIG!

33

WHAT DO YOU WANT TO BE
KNOWN FOR?

(DON'T PLAY SMALL — BE
BOLD IN YOUR DESIRES!)

34

35

transformation comes not by adding things on, but by removing what didn't belong in the first place. we forget there is something perfect already within us.

BARON BAPTISTE

WHAT IS YOUR PERSONAL
PURPOSE BEHIND YOUR
WORK?

WHY DO YOU DO WHAT
YOU DO?

WHY MUST THIS SUCCEED?

39

reflections

41

AT THE CORE OF
EVERY SALE IS
A PERSON.

---

*an individual with
a desire that you
can help fulfill*

As a business owner, in order for a sale to take place, we must first be able to fulfill a perceived need or desire in the eyes of a prospect – provide them with a solution to a real or perceived problem. Once there is agreement that the service you offer is something that they want, a number of factors come into play as reasons why they ultimately choose to (or choose not to) work with you.

Consider that the prospect chooses not to work with you. Perhaps the objection is cost. Maybe they don't feel "ready." There could be something else they feel they need to work on first. Perhaps your personalities clashed. Whatever the reason, the driving force behind this decision is emotion. Humans are brilliant beings, blessed with both intellect and feelings, after all.

It's important to keep in mind that just because we offer a service that individuals need or want – doesn't mean they want it from us. They want to feel confident in their decision to purchase. And emotions help them arrive at that confidence. They want to know that the company they are choosing to work with is trustworthy, that they are cared about, will be treated as an individual, and that they will get the results they are looking for. Remember, people buy from people. Ultimately to enter an agreement with you, your potential client must have an emotional connection with you.

WHO IS YOUR IDEAL CLIENT?
LIST THEIR DEMOGRAPHICS.

WHAT DOES SHE LIKE TO
DO? WHAT MAGAZINES OR
BOOKS DOES SHE READ?
WHERE DOES SHE SHOP?
IS SHE SINGLE? MARRIED?

48 DOES HE HAVE CHILDREN?
WHAT TYPE OF CAREER
DOES SHE HAVE? WHAT ARE
HIS FAVORITE PASTIMES? IS
SHE SPIRITUAL? WHO DOES
SHE FOLLOW IN THE MEDIA?
WHO ARE HIS MENTORS?

GIVE HER A NAME. WRITE
ABOUT HER - TELL HER
STORY.

49

WHAT ARE YOUR IDEAL
CLIENT'S PAIN POINTS?

WHAT KEEPS HER UP AT
NIGHT OR WAKES HIM UP AT
3 AM?

WHAT IS SHE STRUGGLING
50 WITH RIGHT NOW?

51

as we let our
own light
shine,
we unconsciously give
other people the permission
to do
the same.

NELSON MANDELA

WHAT RESULT IS YOUR IDEAL
CLIENT LOOKING FOR?

WHAT "MAGIC PILL" ARE
THEY IN SEARCH OF?

WRITE DOWN KEY PHRASES
THAT YOUR PAST CLIENTS
HAVE USED, OR THINGS YOU
HEAR FROM PROSPECTS.
SPEAK IN THEIR LANGUAGE.

WHAT DO YOU ACTUALLY
HELP YOUR CLIENTS
ACHIEVE?

WHAT ARE THE REAL
RESULTS THAT CLIENTS
EXPERIENCE AFTER
WORKING WITH YOU? [HINT:
56 LOOK AT THE RESULTS
YOUR PAST CLIENTS HAVE
EXPERIENCED.]

DO THESE RESULTS MATCH
WHAT THEY ARE LOOKING
FOR [SEE PREVIOUS
QUESTION]?

note

QUITE OFTEN THE THING YOUR CLIENT IS LOOKING
FOR ISN'T EXACTLY WHAT THEY REALLY NEED.
THIS IS AN IMPORTANT DISTINCTION AND IS A
KEY PIECE OF INFORMATION TO CONSIDER WHEN
SPEAKING ABOUT WHAT YOU DO AND BUILDING
YOUR BRAND PROMISE AND MANIFESTO.

reflections

AT THE CORE OF EVERY BRAND IS **A PERSON.**

---

an intelligent individual with an amazing vision and a desire to impact the lives of other beautiful beings

B

randing can be a confusing concept. Some people think a brand refers to a company logo, or it's identifying visual elements and marks. Some refer to branding as a marketing strategy. Some think branding refers to messaging. The truth is that your brand and brand strategy encompass all of these things.

Entrepreneur magazine states, "Simply put, your brand is your promise to your customer. It tells them what they can expect from your products and services, and it differentiates your offering from that of your competitors. Your brand is derived from who you are, who you want to be, and who people perceive you to be."

If people need an emotional connection to make a purchase, it makes sense that your brand should carry emotion. Your brand should have a voice: a mission and a commitment. It should be distinct and unique, and have a personality. Your brand should stand for something. It should mean something in the eyes of the consumer. And the visual representation of your company should embody the essence of your brand and these emotions as well.

But where does this emotion come from and how is a brand built? It all starts with you. The founder. The intelligent individual with an amazing vision and desire to positively impact the lives of other people.

WHAT IS YOUR COMPANY'S
MISSION?

YOUR MISSION STATEMENT
SHOULD CLAIM YOUR
COMPANY'S CORE PURPOSE
AND WHO YOU SERVE.

66 [HINT: IF YOU'RE STUCK,
TRY USING THIS SIMPLE
FORMULA FOR STARTERS:

"I/WE HELP

_____

BE/DO/HAVE

_____

SO THAT THEY

CAN_____."]

67

WHAT THOUGHTS, FEELINGS, AND EMOTIONS SHOULD BE EVOKED WITHIN YOUR IDEAL CLIENT WHEN THEY VISIT YOUR WEBSITE OR HAVE A CONVERSATION WITH YOU?

68   MAKE A LIST OF SOME KEY ADJECTIVES YOU'D USE TO DESCRIBE YOUR BRAND.

note

NOTICE HOW THIS LIST COMPARES TO THE ONE YOU
CREATED ABOUT YOUR OWN SELF ON PAGE 25.

only as deep
as i look
can i see

only as big as i
dream
can i be.

KAREN RAVN

reflections

IS YOUR VISUAL BRANDING CONSISTENT ACROSS ALL MARKETING MATERIALS AND VISUAL ELEMENTS WHERE YOUR BRAND IS FEATURED? [WEBSITE, BUSINESS CARDS, ADVERTISING, SALES COLLATERAL, SALES PAGES, PRODUCTS, EVENT COLLATERAL, EMAIL SIGNATURES, POWERPOINT TEMPLATES, FREE REPORTS, EVERYWHERE]

☐ YES   ☐ NO

DO YOU HAVE A CONSISTENT BRAND MESSAGE?

☐ YES   ☐ NO

ARE PEOPLE TALKING ABOUT YOU/YOUR COMPANY AND IF SO, DO YOU LIKE WHAT THEY ARE SAYING?

☐ YES   ☐ NO

DO YOU LIKE YOUR BRAND AND WHAT IT STANDS FOR?

☐ YES   ☐ NO

DO YOU LIKE THE VISUAL ELEMENTS OF YOUR BRAND AND/OR LOGO?

☐ YES   ☐ NO

DOES YOUR LOGO AND THE VISUAL REPRESENTATION OF YOUR BRAND RESONATE WITH YOU, YOUR MESSAGE, AND YOUR CLIENTS?

☐ YES   ☐ NO

reflections

note

IMAGINE YOU ARE THE HOST OF AN EXQUISITE GALA, OR AN INTIMATE BACKYARD CELEBRATION ON THE COAST – WHICHEVER MAKES YOUR SOUL SMILE. THE EVENT EXUDES YOUR BRANDING AND STYLE – FROM THE DECOR TO THE FOOD, THE AROMA TO THE AMBIANCE. EVERYONE YOU CARE ABOUT MOST IS THERE AND THEY ARE HAVING A WONDERFUL TIME. YOU'VE CREATED THIS BEAUTIFUL EXPERIENCE FOR THEM AS IF IT WERE A PEEK INTO YOUR MOST AUTHENTIC SELF. LET THAT FEELING SOAK IN FOR A MOMENT... NOW, IMAGINE IF YOU COULD CREATE THAT SAME FEELING FOR EVERY VISITOR TO YOUR WEBSITE. POWERFUL, RIGHT? THAT'S THE IMPACT OF AUTHENTIC BRANDING. IT'S ALL ABOUT THE EXPERIENCE.

AT THE CORE OF
EVERY AUTHORITY,
EVERY EXPERT,
EVERY CELEBRITY
IS **A PERSON.**

---

a person,

just like you

and me

As humans, we are fascinated by experts. Somehow, it seems to us that just because someone is labeled as an expert in a particular field, she must be an amazing super-human with capabilities far beyond our own. We turn to these experts for their knowledge, but soon become even more interested in what makes them different. We want to know more about their personality, their struggles, their triumphs, their everyday lives.

The same is true for celebrities. Their success gives them visibility in the public eye – and soon that success matters far less than what they do with their time off, who they do it with, where they spend vacations, how many children they have, or if they're helping children in need.

Humans crave connection. Knowing personal details about these experts and celebrities somehow makes us feel more connected to them, as if we share something with them.

80

Think about this: if a potential client (a person) had someone they could connect with as the face of your brand (a person), how much more powerful could your brand be, and how many more lives could you impact? Infusing the essence of you and what makes you different, what you stand for, and who you are into your branding provides an instant human connection for people to identify with.

WHAT CELEBRITIES AND EXPERTS DO YOU MOST IDENTIFY WITH AND WHY?

....

....

....

....

....

....

....

....

....

....

....

....

....

DOES KNOWING PERSONAL DETAILS ABOUT THESE CELEBRITIES AND EXPERTS
MAKE YOU FEEL MORE CONNECTED TO THEM?

☐ YES   ☐ NO

it takes
courage
to grow up
& become

who you really are.

E.E. CUMMINGS

WHAT ARE YOU BRILLIANT
AT?

WHAT SETS YOU APART
FROM OTHERS IN YOUR
FIELD?

WHAT IS UNIQUE ABOUT YOU
AND YOUR OFFERINGS?

HOW WOULD YOU FEEL IF
CLIENTS CAME TO YOU
PURELY BECAUSE OF THE
PERSON YOU ARE AND WHAT
YOU STAND FOR? WHAT
OTHER FEELINGS DOES THIS
POSSIBILITY BRING UP FOR
YOU?

88

HOW CAN YOU CARRY THAT
THROUGH THE ENTIRE
BRAND CULTURE OF YOUR
COMPANY?

89

the privilege of a lifetime is being who you are.

reflections

93

YOU AS
A PERSON.

---

you as
your brand

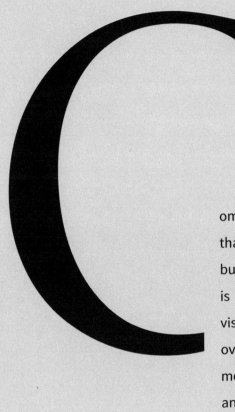

Coming to the realization that, as a service-based business owner your brand is more powerful with you visibly at it's core, can be overwhelming and scary. It means that you will be seen and heard. No more hiding behind your desk, business name, or website.

But it also can be so liberating! Go back and read the reasons why you started your business (page 18). What was your big vision? Now read the results your clients experience after working with you (page 56). It's time to get back in touch with the beautiful person you are.

Choosing to grow your business and stand firmly at it's core as an advocate causes you to really examine who you are at *your* core. Being clear on your true mission and purpose means accepting and loving yourself just as you are – imperfections and all. Although this often proves to be a healing process for the individual, the greater impact falls on your clients.

By choosing to follow your purpose today, think of how many lives you will impact tomorrow!

whatever is given to you
on the day you
are born,
you are the one
who decides who
you will become
every day.
beauty grows
as we grow
into ourselves.

GARANCE DORÉ

YOUR EVOLUTION
AS **A PERSON.**

_____

*the evolution
of your brand*

reflections

THE EXCELLENT WORK THAT YOU'VE DONE IN THE PRECEDING PAGES IS JUST THE BEGINNING FOR YOUR BRAND. WE ARE CONSTANTLY EVOLVING AS INDIVIDUALS AND AS BRANDS. CONTINUE BRAINSTORMING IN THE PAGES THAT FOLLOW. USE THIS SPACE TO CAPTURE YOUR THOUGHTS AND ASPIRATIONS. REMEMBER TO DREAM AND EMBRACE YOUR DESIRES! YOU CAN ACHIEVE WHATEVER YOU PUT YOUR MIND TO - IF YOU ARE CLEAR ON WHAT YOU WANT, AND TAKE SMALL STEPS EACH DAY TOWARD THAT GOAL. YOU ARE MORE POWERFUL THAN YOU KNOW, AND YOU ARE LOVED BEYOND MEASURE.

105

107

109

110

111

112

113

your vision
will become clear
only when you look into your
heart. who looks
outside,
dreams
who looks inside,
awakens.

CARL JUNG

A

re you feeling a little more confident? Are you starting to see the incredible person inside of you? It is my hope that this journal has given you a loving nudge to move more confidently in the direction of your true purpose. To show a little bit of vulnerability. To step out in a much bigger way, reach even more people, and make a greater impact on the world.

Want more? How you express your brand is just as important as what you're expressing. Identify your unique style with our fun (and free!) assessment at *yourbrandstylequiz.com*.

Your mission is too valuable not to give it a meaningful brand and style.

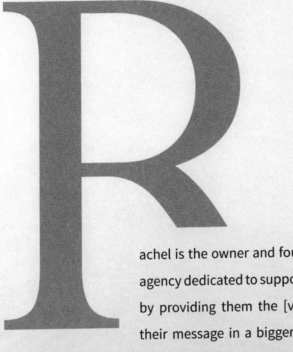

Rachel is the owner and founder of Brand Therapy, a creative agency dedicated to supporting mission-driven entrepreneurs by providing them the [visual] confidence to communicate their message in a bigger, more beautiful way. She believes that by allowing your unique style to shine through in your brand, you can connect with others on a deeper and more emotional level. At Brand Therapy, we are passionate about helping women build their self-confidence and self-love through visual expression.

You can learn more at *yourbrandtherapy.com*.